796.332 Aaseng, Nate
Aa
        Football's most
    shocking upsets

★★★ Football's ★★★
MOST SHOCKING
UPSETS

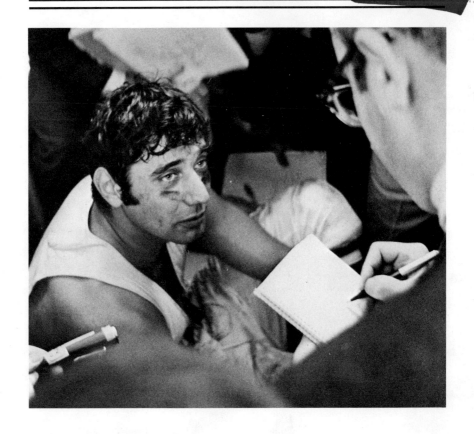

★★★ *Football's* ★★★
MOST SHOCKING
UPSETS

Nate Aaseng

Lerner Publications Company
Minneapolis

Front cover: Dallas Cowboy tackle Randy White (54) vents his frustrations on San Francisco quarterback Joe Montana (16).
Back cover: Top left: A swarming Detroit Lion defense devours Vince Lonbardi's "invincible" 1962 unit. Bottom left: Mike Wood's inability to kick the Oilers while they were down would come to haunt the Chargers. Right: Dwight Clark's famous stretch in the 1981 NFL title game brought the Cowboys painful memories of an earlier embarrassment.
Page 1: A funny thing happened to the Baltimore Colts on the way to their Super Bowl III title—just as Joe Namath had predicted.
Page 2: Even football's most nearly perfect team, the 1962 Green Bay Packers, wasn't immune to the upset, a point that Detroit's Roger Brown (76) impresses upon a fumbling Bart Starr (15).

To Linda

Library of Congress Cataloging-in-Publication Data

Aaseng, Nathan.
  Football's most shocking upsets.

  (Sports talk)
  Summary: Profiles eight championship games in the National Football League, in which superior playing and plain luck resulted in wins for teams expected to lose.
  1. National Football League—History—Juvenile literature. [1. National Football League—History. 2. Football—History] I. Title. II. Series.
  GV955.5.N35A27   1986   796.332'78   84-23322
  ISBN: 0-8225-1529-6 (lib. bdg.)

Manufactured in the United States of America

1 2 3 4 5 6 7 8 9 10 96 95 94 93 92 91 90 89 88 87 86

★★★ Contents ★★★

All football teams are *not* created equal. In Tampa Bay's early days, Ricky Bell (42) would have faced better odds entering a state lottery than trying to beat these Pittsburgh Steelers!

Introduction

Rooting for the underdog is one of the most popular traditions in the sports world. Most fans feel drawn into cheering for a less-talented team to upset the favorites. Upsets add the key element of suspense to athletic competition and break up the monotony of seeing the same people on top game after game.

To hear some National Football League (NFL) spokesmen tell it, however, you would think there wasn't much room for memorable upsets in pro football, the sport that first used the phrase, "On any given day, any team in the league can beat any other." The NFL is proud of the fact that most of its teams are competitive. If you don't believe that the NFL is well-balanced, try to pick all the winners in any weekend of NFL action. Even the experts rarely succeed at that.

With such balance, how can such shocking upsets occur? As unlikely as it may seem, pro football has provided as many thrilling upset moments as any other sport. There are at least four reasons why:

1. The NFL's balance of competition is misleading. Through the years, the league has had its share of super teams and pushovers. Was it really true that *any* team could beat the 1962 Packers, the 1976 Steelers, or the unbeaten 1972 Dolphins? A person could grow mighty old waiting for that to happen! What were the chances of the winless Tampa Bay Bucs beating *anyone* in 1976?

2. With fewer games on its schedule than most pro sports, pro football makes each game more memorable. An upset can't be truly shocking during the regular season in baseball, hockey, or basketball because there isn't enough tension. But in football, each game is crucial. A loss to a poor team can easily knock a team out of the play-offs, and such a disaster will stick in the minds of fans for years.

3. Emotion can play a big part in a football game. Through sheer will power, a weak team can push around a better team that isn't as mentally ready to play.

4. Luck can play a big part in a football game. In the most famous upsets, the differences between favorites and underdogs are so great that the underdogs need luck to pull them through. Fumbles, penalties, and slips are all part of football. Even a bad team is tough to beat when all the breaks go in their favor.

This book is about eight of the most unbelievable upsets in NFL history. Such stars as Joe Namath, Fran Tarkenton, Fred Dean, and Russ Francis will show how they helped pull off their mysterious wins against the most incredible odds.

Frigid playing conditions frequently numbed Minnesota Viking opponents who ventured into Metropolitan Stadium. None of their foes, however, left town in such total shock as the Chicago Bears in 1961 (see chapter 2).

NFL fans predicted that Cleveland quarterback Otto Graham would lose more than just his helmet when he tried to move the ball against a *real* defense!

★★★1★★★
Welcome to the NFL

Cleveland Browns vs. Philadelphia Eagles
September 16, 1950

National Football League officials in the late 1940s insisted there was only one *real* professional football league. Sure, the new All-American Football Conference claimed to play pro football, but why would fans waste time and money on such a rag-tag outfit? The AAFC, organized in 1946, had barely survived through four seasons. As far as the NFL was concerned, its only accomplishment was to cost owners more money in the bidding for college stars. Feeling the money pinch, the NFL teams agreed to accept three AAFC teams into their league for the 1950 season. They expected the addition of the Cleveland Browns, the San Francisco 49ers, and the Baltimore Colts to eliminate competition for players and to provide easy wins for NFL teams as well.

The ridicule from the NFL had been hard to take, especially for the proud Browns. Coached by inventive Paul Brown, Cleveland had romped to a 52-4-3 record over the four years of play, winning all four AAFC titles. Quarterback Otto Graham had thrown the ball well, and 238-pound fullback Marion Motley had run for six yards per carry. But Cleveland's impressive statistics didn't erase the sneers. "It's easy to look good when playing a bunch of nobodies," NFL backers said. "Wait until they face a *real* football team."

There was no doubt that Cleveland would face a "real" football team in their first game of the 1950 season when they happened to draw the defending champion Philadelphia Eagles for their first NFL opponent.

No one suspected that Graham would go on to become the top-rated passer in NFL history.

The Eagles, loaded with huge, powerful men, had perfected the 5-4 defense. This defense, which centered on five bruising linemen, had totally stifled opponents in the past two NFL games. In 1948, Philadelphia had allowed the Chicago Bears only 35 yards passing and 96 rushing in posting a 7-0 win. The following year, they had held the explosive Los Angeles Rams to 98 yards passing and 21 rushing in another shutout win. Incredibly, the Eagles had allowed these strong foes only 13 first downs in the two games combined!

Still, those championship games had been nothing out of the ordinary for the Eagles. During the 1949 season, they had allowed the fewest points, passing yards, and total yards in the NFL. At the same time, their offense led the league in rushing yardage, with Steve Van Buren capturing his third straight rushing title. Philadelphia could also move through the air with Tommy Thompson, the NFL's number-two passer, throwing to his fine end, Pete Pihos. The Eagles' only worry going into the game was that Van Buren was out with an injury.

Above: Steve Van Buren. Below: Tommy Thompson.

More than 71,000 fans crammed into the stadium to watch their home team smash the Browns on September 16, 1950. Since the contest had been moved up to Saturday night instead of Sunday afternoon, the rest of the league also tuned in on the action.

The game started poorly for the Browns. First, there was the heartbreak of having a 64-yard punt return called back because of a clipping penalty. Then, the Eagles grabbed the lead with a 15-yard field goal.

The Browns, however, had been studying the Eagles for four years while waiting for a chance to play them, and they had discovered that the 5-4 defense left an open spot just behind the middle of the Eagle line. Cleveland would be sure to throw to that area often. They also saw that, although they were strong, the Eagles weren't quick. If the Browns spaced their blockers far apart, the Eagles would have to spread out as well. And that would give each of the slower Eagle linemen too much area to cover.

Trailing 3-0, Cleveland turned loose their fine stable of pass catchers. With perfect protection from his blockers, Otto Graham waited for Dub Jones to

Dante Lavelli lunges out of the grasp of a grounded Eagle for a first-half score.

break into the clear. Jones grabbed Graham's pass and broke through the defenders for 59 yards and a touchdown. Even the most stubborn NFL fans had to admit that it was as pretty a play as they had seen in their own league.

The Brown defense then turned back Philadelphia's famed running attack. Although Marion Motley was better known for his punishing runs, he could also play ferociously on defense. He and middle guard Bill Willis shut down the Eagles and turned the ball back to their offense.

Mixing Motley's powerful bursts with precision passes, Graham again guided his team downfield. From the 26-yard line, he saw wide receiver Dante Lavelli racing for the end zone. His pass was too long, but Lavelli dove through the end zone to grab it for the score. The half ended with the score 14-3 in favor of Cleveland.

The uneasy Eagle fans had been waiting for something to cheer about throughout the half. Thanks to Graham's sharp passes, however, the game began to be downright depressing. Five straight completions in the third quarter brought the Browns to the Eagle 12. Then

Even before he had the ball tucked away, Mac Speedie was looking for a way past the Eagles' Tom Scott.

Philadelphia's pass rush finally broke through, but Graham dodged the linemen until a receiver could get open. This time, it was Mac Speedie's turn, and he caught the pass that put his team ahead, 21-3. Philadelphia tried to make a game of it and closed to 21-10

on a 17-yard toss to Pete Pihos. But they became bogged down so badly on offense that even quarterback Thompson was finally yanked from the lineup.

Having left the Eagles open mouthed with precise pass patterns, the Browns set out to prove they could run the ball as well. The spread-out line of the Eagles was no match for the quicker Browns, and Cleveland rammed home two more touchdowns to finish off a convincing 35 to 10 win.

Not even the die-hard Eagle fans could pretend the win had all been a matter of luck. Graham had shredded the Philadelphia defense for 346 yards, with 21 completions in 38 throws. The Browns had added 141 yards running to outgain the Eagles by a total of 487 to 262. After four years of scorn from pro football fans, the Browns had needed only one game to show they were one of the best teams in football.

How times have changed! Wearing a lineman's number and shoes that might embarrass any modern player, Graham completed an upset season by leading his team to a 30-28 win over the Rams in the 1950 title game.

HOW THE BROWNS UPSET THE EAGLES

September 16, 1950
Connie Mack Stadium, Philadelphia
Attendance: 71,237

	Philadelphia Eagles	Cleveland Browns
Previous Year's Record:	11-1	Not in NFL
Returning All-Pros:	Pete Pihos (end) Vic Sears (t) Steve Van Buren (rb)	Did not play in NFL

	1	2	3	4	FINAL
Cleveland Browns	7	7	7	14	35
Philadelphia Eagles	3	0	0	7	10

Eagles	Cliff Patton	15-yard field goal
Browns	Dub Jones	59-yard pass from Otto Graham (Forrest Grigg kick)
Browns	Dante Lavelli	26-yard pass from Otto Graham (Forrest Grigg kick)
Browns	Mac Speedie	13-yard pass from Otto Graham (Forrest Grigg kick)
Eagles	Pete Pihos	17-yard pass from Bill Mackrides (Cliff Patton kick)
Browns	Otto Graham	1-yard run (Forrest Grigg kick)
Browns	Rex Bumgardner	2-yard run (Forrest Grigg kick)

		Browns	Eagles
First Downs		23	24
Yardage:	Rushing	141	148
	Passing	346	118
	Total	487	266
	Penalized	98	48
Passing:	Completions	21	11
	Attempts	38	37
	Interceptions	2	3
Fumbles Lost		2	2

Outstanding Performance: Brown quarterback Otto Graham completed 21 of 38 passes for 346 yards and three touchdowns and ran for another score.

Subpar Performance: Eagle quarterback Tommy Thompson was taken out in favor of quarterback Bill Mackrides.

The Viking linemen may be slow—Tommy Mason (20) has given up waiting for them— but they were always ready to pop someone and proved to the Bears that hard hitting can sometimes overcome superior talent.

2

No Respect for Their Elders

Minnesota Vikings vs. Chicago Bears
September 17, 1961

"They're not big, but they sure are slow!" That was a common description of the National Football League's newest team in 1961, the Minnesota Vikings. Any new entry let into the league had to pay the price of starting with a miserable team. Along with a few draft choices, the other clubs allowed them to fill their rosters with rejects and benchwarmers from around the league. No one expected them to be competitive. Just trying to survive in the first year would be challenge enough.

The Dallas Cowboys had just limped through their first season in 1960. As expected, they had not won a game all year. It took them until the second-to-last game of the season before they managed to gain a tie, 31-31, with the New York Giants. Now it was the Vikings'

turn to provide easy victories for the established teams.

The Vikings did have a shrewd and inventive coach named Norm Van Brocklin. Having just finished quarterbacking the Philadelphia Eagles to the NFL title in 1960, Van Brocklin knew what it would take to win. He also had a sprinkling of respected veterans on the team. Players like halfback Hugh McElhenny and quarterback George Shaw had enjoyed fine careers in the league, but, unfortunately, their careers were fading quickly. Shaw, who had started for the New York Giants during much of 1960, seemed near the end of the line after a week of pre-season showing. As expected, the Vikings did not win a game during the exhibition play.

Viking coach Norm Van Brocklin (above) could no longer do it all himself as he had once done with the Rams (right), but he knew how to get the most out of mediocre players.

As their first regular-season opponent, the Vikings happened to draw the Chicago Bears, the NFL's oldest member. Deep in tradition and talent, the Bears had pounded the Vikings, 30-7, in one of the later exhibition games. Although they had slipped to 5-6-1 the previous year, the Bears were poised again to challenge for the title. They had strength-

Left: Aging running back Hugh McElhenny gave Minnesota its only link to respectability. Right: With the arrival of Billy Wade from the Rams, the Bears hoped to field an offense to go with their savage defense.

ened one of their weakest positions, quarterback, by trading for Billy Wade of the Los Angeles Rams. Wade had been the league's fourth-ranked passer in 1960. Along with rugged Rick Casares and flashy Willie Gallimore in the backfield, Chicago had plenty of scoring punch.

As always, the Bears' defense was even stronger than their offense. The hard-hitting Bears were led by 6-foot, 8-inch Doug Atkins and three of the most ferocious linebackers in the league: Bill George, Larry Morris, and Joe Fortunato. Especially strong against the pass, they had allowed only 14 touchdown passes in 1960. Their record of allowing only 1,801 yards passing had topped the NFL. All in all, it was a powerful club that was only a couple of years away from winning the championship.

Linebackers such as Larry Morris (left) and Joe Fortunato (right) carried on a Bear tradition of punishing opponents as well as defeating them.

The Bears expected to fatten their statistics against the Vikings when they traveled to Minnesota for the opening game. No one believed it would take much of an effort for the Bears to win, and, at first, the Bears did not seem to be putting forth much effort. They played sloppily in the first half, fumbling the ball twice and having a pass intercepted. They even gave the Vikings two points when their center sailed the ball so far over his punter's head that it went into the stands!

Despite this, there was little cause for concern. The Vikings, led by quarterback Shaw, could not take advantage of Chicago's careless mistakes. Despite playing about as poorly as they were capable of, the Bears still led the game.

As the Viking offense floundered late into the second period, Van Brocklin decided it was time for a change. Since the team could not be playing much worse, he figured there was nothing to lose by sending in their rookie third-round draft choice from Georgia to play quarterback. The youngster, Fran Tarkenton, replaced Shaw, and quickly things began to happen. Tarkenton had an unusual style of play for that era. Instead of standing still while looking for a pass receiver and getting pounded by the pass rush, Fran would run for his life. He could throw on the run, and he even seemed to enjoy running the ball himself.

The Bears were not quite prepared for this spunky newcomer. It took Tarkenton only a few minutes to drive the Vikings downfield toward their first touchdown. Fran finished off the march with a 14-yard pass to Bob Schnelker.

Fran's play more amused than impressed the experts. The Viking score had provided a little excitement for Minnesota fans, but, they guessed, it would probably only arouse the Bears into playing decent football. The game was expected to turn into a rout in the second half.

The Bears didn't believe they had anything to fear from this undersized rookie out of Georgia named Francis Tarkenton.

That's exactly what happened, only it was the Vikings who were running all over the Chicago Bears! Tarkenton seemed unstoppable as he pierced the proud Chicago defense again and again. Spreading the glory around among his teammates, Fran threw touchdown passes to running back McElhenny and wide receiver Jerry Reichow in the third period. In the fourth, he found wide receiver Dave Middleton open in the end zone for another score. To top off his incredible performance, Tarkenton ran for a fifth touchdown on his own!

The Bears left the field in a stupor, soundly beaten by a score of 37 to 13! In his first pro game, Fran Tarkenton had completed 17 of 23 passes for 250 yards and four touchdowns, all against a top pass defense. Never has a new pro team started so impressively. The Vikings actually proved to be nearly as bad as everyone had thought, as they won only 2 of their final 11 games. But their unbelievable first win showed the danger of taking *any* team too lightly.

Perhaps the Bears might have felt a little better if they'd known they had been done in by a Hall of Famer who would wind up with more completions, more passing yardage, and more touchdown passes than any other player in NFL history.

HOW THE VIKINGS UPSET THE BEARS

September 17, 1961
Metropolitan Stadium, Bloomington
Attendance: 32,236

	Chicago Bears	Minnesota Vikings
Previous Year's Record:	5-6-1	Not in NFL
Returning All-Pros:	Stan Jones (g)	None
	Doug Atkins (de)	
	Bill George (lb)	

	1	2	3	4	FINAL
Chicago Bears	0	6	0	7	**13**
Minnesota Vikings	3	7	14	13	**37**

Vikings	Mike Mercer	12-yard field goal
Vikings	Bill Schnelker	14-yard pass from Fran Tarkenton (Mike Mercer kick)
Bears	Rick Casares	2-yard run (kick failed)
Vikings	Jerry Reichow	29-yard pass from Fran Tarkenton (Mike Mercer kick)
Vikings	Hugh McElhenny	2-yard pass from Fran Tarkenton (Mike Mercer kick)
Vikings	Fran Tarkenton	3-yard run (Mike Mercer kick)
Vikings	Dave Middleton	2-yard pass from Fran Tarkenton (kick blocked)
Bears	Willie Galimore	10-yard pass from Billy Wade (Roger Laclerc kick)

		Bears	Vikings
First Downs		20	17
Yardage:	Rushing	134	79
	Passing	146	250
	Total	280	329
	Penalized	33	53
Passing:	Completions	8	17
	Attempts	17	23
	Interceptions	4	0
Fumbles Lost		1	1

Outstanding Performance: Viking quarterback Fran Tarkenton completed 17 of 23 passes for 250 yards and four touchdowns, ran for another score, and threw no interceptions.

Subpar Performance: Bear quarterback Billy Wade completed only 8 of 17 passes with four interceptions.

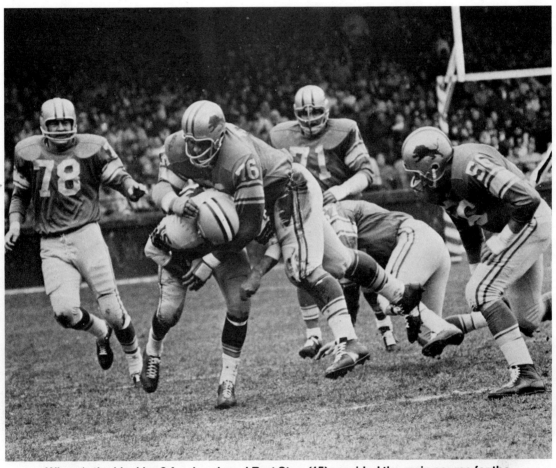

Where's the blocking? An abandoned Bart Starr (15) provided the main course for the Lions' Thanksgiving Day feast. Here Detroit's enormous tackle Roger Brown (76) helps himself to the quarterback while his teammates arrive to clean up the leftovers.

★★★ 3 ★★★

The Lions' Thanksgiving Feast

Detroit Lions vs. Green Bay Packers
November 22, 1962

The Green Bay Packers had much to be thankful for on Thanksgiving Day, 1962. Coach Vince Lombardi had molded them into the most powerful football squad in NFL history. Defeat was only a distant memory to the Packers, a team that had won their last 18 games. As their 37-0 pasting of a strong New York Giant team in the 1961 title game had shown, there wasn't a team close to matching them. During the 1962 season, they had won all 10 of their games and had blown away their opponents by a combined score of 299 to 74.

Preparing a game plan against Green Bay was like trying to decide how to put out a dozen fires with one bucket of water. The Packers ranked number one in both defense and offense. Hard-nosed fullback Jim Taylor was leading the NFL in both rushing and scoring.

If you stopped him, Green Bay could turn to the league's top passer, Bart Starr. Most likely, you wouldn't get a good shot at either one, however, since four of Green Bay's five offensive linemen were headed for the Hall of Fame.

If by some fluke the offense bogged down, Green Bay's defense could squeeze the life out of its foes. With a generous sprinking of All-Pros at all positions, the Packers were especially stingy against the pass. Willie Wood led the league with eight interceptions, and Herb Adderley was tied for second with seven.

The Detroit Lions were one team that could possibly make the Packers work up a sweat. With a stubborn defense led by tackle Alex Karras, linebacker Joe Schmidt, and cornerback Richard "Night Train" Lane, they had recorded

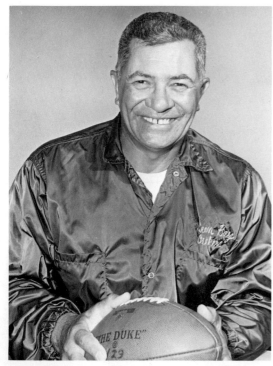

"When he tells me to sit, I don't look for a chair!" said Packer Henry Jordan of coach Vince Lombardi (above). In 1962, the Packers came close to the perfection their coach demanded.

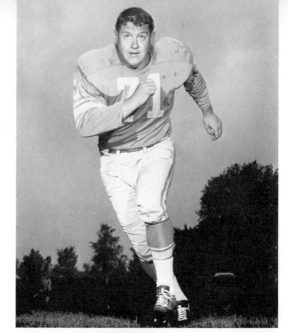

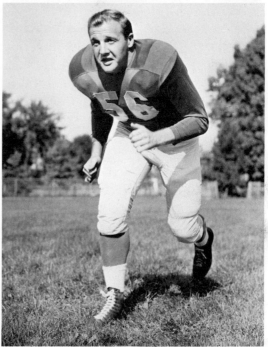

The Lions leaned heavily on defensive standouts Alex Karras (top), Joe Schmidt (bottom), Night Train Lane (p. 29, top), and Wayne Walker (p. 29, bottom) to make up for an average defense.

an 8-2 mark going into the game. Their offense, guided by quarterback Milt Plum, didn't overwhelm anyone, but they often scored enough points to win.

Detroit had also hired a clever defensive coach named Don Shula. In preparing for the Packers, Shula showed the attention to detail that would later make him one of the most successful head coaches in the NFL. He came up

with a plan to throw the disciplined Packers off guard. First, to confuse Green Bay blockers, the linemen and linebackers were to jump around just before the play started. Secondly, they wanted to take away the quick pass. Shula instructed linebacker Wayne Walker to drift in front of Packer wide receiver

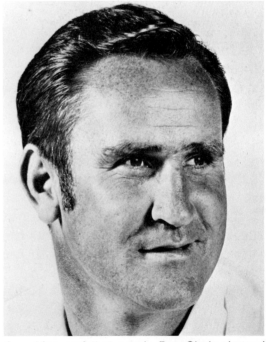

As a Lion assistant coach, Don Shula showed early signs of the intelligence that would lead him to a record six Super Bowl appearances as a head coach.

Max McGee while defensive back Dick LeBeau played behind him. With McGee covered on short patterns, Starr would have to pause to find another receiver. That would allow time for the Lion's final strategy, an all-out pass rush, to overrun the blockers.

Along with the 57,000 fans crammed into the stadium, millions of television viewers pulled themselves away from their Thanksgiving dinners to watch the action. Most of them hoped the Lions could keep it interesting for awhile. The first clue that something strange might happen took place early in the first quarter. After the Lions stopped Green Bay's first offensive series, Packer punter Boyd Dowler flubbed a punt. It traveled only 15 yards and gave Detroit excellent field position.

Then, faced with a third and four at the Packer 34, the Lions fooled the veteran Green Bay defense. With the Packers expecting a short pass, Detroit's Gail Cogdill slipped behind Herb Adderley. Milt Plum lofted a pass to him, and Cogdill raced into the end zone for a 7-0 lead.

That score seemed to unleash an avalanche against the Packers. For the rest of the first half, the Lion front four of Karras, Roger Brown, Darris McCord, and Sam Williams buried the finest offensive line in the game. Leading the charge was tackle Roger Brown, an incredibly quick 296-pounder. Coach Lombardi later said it wasn't a matter of his Packers not being ready to play; he simply had never seen a defensive line burst across the line of scrimmage that quickly. As if the Packer blockers didn't have their hands full, Joe Schmidt roared in on frequent blitzes from his middle linebacker spot. Packer quarterback Starr could not hit the short pass because of Detroit's double coverage, and he wasn't yet polished in the art of the screen pass over the rush. As a result, he was sacked time after time deep in his own backfield.

With Lion fans howling in surprise and delight at the Lions' manhandling of the Packer offense, Detroit's offense came to life. Plum called for another long pass to Cogdill. This time, Adderley matched the Lion receiver stride for stride, but the pass was perfect. Cogdill snatched it away from Adderley for 27 yards and another touchdown.

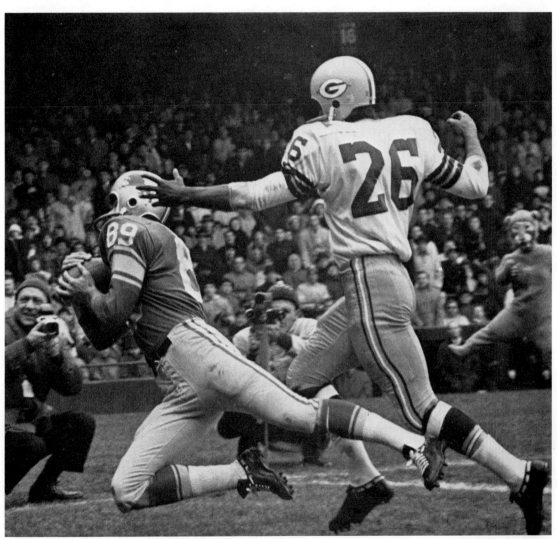

Gail Cogdill's spectacular effort beats perfect coverage by Green Bay's All-Pro cornerback Herb Adderley (26) for a 14-0 Lion lead.

It was then that Roger Brown set up shop in the Packer backfield. While Star backpedaled to set up for a pass, he felt Brown pile into him. The Lion tackled Starr 15 yards behind the line and forced him to fumble. Brown's linemate, Sam Williams, scooped up the loose ball and dashed the final six yards for another Lion touchdown.

Trailing 21 to 0, Green Bay's offense took the field only to see Brown break through again. Roaring in so quickly that none of the Packers could even attempt a block, Brown trapped Starr in the end zone for a safety. The two points gave Detroit a 23 to 0 lead.

Some of the Packer stars responded to their misery with characteristic good humor. They later liked to tell the story of how Bart Starr was trying to choose a play when things were at their worst. One by one, Starr's aching teammates told him that, if it was all the same with him, they would rather not have to carry the ball. Finally Max McGee suggested that he throw a long pass and, that way, no one would get hurt!

The statistics from that first half seemed like something out of science fiction. The unbeatable Packers were 23 points behind. In 30 minutes of play, Starr had been sacked eight times for 76 yards in losses. The NFL's top runner, Taylor, had been stopped cold with eight carries for -3 yards!

The Lions were content to protect their huge lead after increasing their margin to 26-0 in the second half. Although Green Bay did close the final gap to 26-14, their offense never did move on the Lions. One Packer touchdown was scored by the defense; the other set up by a fumble recovery at the Lion 14.

The Packer offensive totals for the day showed 73 yards rushing and 59 passing. Starr had spent most of the game prying Detroit linemen off his back. The famous Packer blocking had crumbled in allowing 11 sacks. Counting the 15 yards Starr had lost before fumbling and the 7 he had lost on the safety, Green Bay lost 109 yards attempting to pass! Rarely has such a mighty team fallen so low. Green Bay went on to win another NFL title that year, but on that one afternoon, even the seemingly indestructable Packers had proved they were only human.

HOW THE LIONS UPSET THE PACKERS

November 22, 1962
Tiger Stadium, Detroit
Attendance: 57,598

	Detroit Lions	**Green Bay Packers**
1962 Record Prior to Game:	10-0	8-2
1962 All-Pros:	Roger Brown (dt)	Ron Kramer (te)
	Alex Karras (dt)	Fuzzy Thurston (g)
	Joe Schmidt (lb)	Jerry Kramer (g)
	Yale Lary (db-punter)	Jim Ringo (c)
		Forrest Gregg (t)
		Jim Taylor (rb)
		Willie Davis (de)
		Henry Jordan (dt)
		Dan Currie (lb)
		Bill Forrester (lb)
		Herb Adderley (db)

	1	2	3	4	FINAL
Green Bay Packers	0	0	0	14	**14**
Detroit Lions	7	16	3	0	**26**

Lions	Gail Cogdill	33-yard pass from Milt Plum (Wayne Walker kick)
Lions	Gail Cogdill	27-yard pass from Milt Plum (Wayne Walker kick)
Lions	Sam Williams	6-yard fumble return (Wayne Walker kick)
Lions	Roger Brown	tackled Bart Starr in end zone
Lions	Milt Plum	47-yard field goal
Packers	Willie Davis	fumble recovery in end zone (Jerry Kramer kick)
Packers	Jim Taylor	4-yard run (Jerry Kramer kick)

		Packers	**Lions**
First Downs		11	14
Yardage:	Rushing	73	153
	Passing	59	147
	Total	132	300
	Penalized	25	59
Passing:	Completions	11	10
	Attempts	19	18
	Interceptions	2	2
Fumbles Lost		3	3

Outstanding Performances: Detroit defensive tackle Roger Brown caused a fumble that resulted in a touchdown and recorded a safety. Detroit wide receiver Gail Cogdill caught three passes for 79 yards and two touchdowns.

Subpar Performance: NFL's leading rusher running back Jim Taylor was held to 47 yards in 13 carries.

Neither the Colts nor Cleveland stars Vince Costello (50), Gary Collins (86), and Frank Ryan (13) can quite believe what is happening in this championship game.

★★★ 4 ★★★

The Defenseless Browns

Baltimore Colts vs. Cleveland Browns
December 27, 1964

To hear the experts hoot and snicker, you'd think the Cleveland Browns had only won the NFL's 1964 Eastern Division title because no one else wanted it. No one had seemed impressed by Cleveland's 10-3-1 record during the regular season. There had been too many glaring weaknesses for the Browns to be considered serious championship material. If you ran your fingers down the NFL's team defensive statistics, you would wonder how the Browns had even survived the season.

Cleveland couldn't stop anyone and gave up more yards and more first downs than any other team in the league. Their defensive problems were the result of a true team effort: the Browns needed help at *all* defensive positions! The defensive backs were too small and slow to keep up with its

meager 28 sacks of the year. The linebackers practically had footprints on their backs from being trampled by opposing runners. As a result, the Browns ranked dead last in defending against the run.

Cleveland's opponents in the 1964 title game, the Baltimore Colts, could hardly wait to start racing each other to the Brown's goal line. The 12-2 Colts expected easy pickings for their explosive offense, which had topped the NFL in points. With a balanced attack that had gained over 3,000 yards passing and over 2,000 rushing, the Colts could take turns high-stepping over the Browns.

Recharged running back Lenny Moore led the Colt attack. Early in the season, Baltimore had tried to trade away their aging star but could find no takers.

35

Lenny Moore's ability to catch the long pass coming out of the backfield gave Baltimore an explosive option in their attack.

off far better linemen than the Browns could throw at them in this game.

Not that Cleveland was totally helpless. No one has ever run with more power and speed than their fullback Jim Brown. Fresh off his seventh rushing

Moore had responded by leading the NFL in touchdowns with 20! Quarterback Johnny Unitas had enjoyed his usual brilliant season, throwing to such sure-handed men as Raymond Berry. In past championship matches, guard Jim Parker and his fellow linemen had held

title in the last eight years, Brown could provide a challenge for the fine Colt defense. Rookie wide receiver Paul Warfield also gave Cleveland a speedy pass-catching threat. But even if Brown and friends could score three or four

In their 12 seasons together in Baltimore, John Unitas (across) and Raymond Berry (above) connected on more completions than any passing duo before them.

touchdowns against a defense that allowed the fewest points in 1964, they would be hard-pressed to make up for their terrible defense.

Cleveland coach Blanton Collier had two weeks to think about this championship mismatch that had made his Browns seven-point underdogs in their own stadium. In an unusual move for that late in the year, he ordered his team back to basic workouts for one week. The Cleveland squad sweated out hard tackling and blocking drills, just like they had gone through in the pre-season. Collier hoped their practices would clean up some of the Browns' sloppy play. But he also need a new play to beat the more talented Colts.

Cleveland defensive backs Bernie Parrish, Ross Fichtner, Walter Beach, and Larry Benz had played far back of the line to guard against long passes. It had been a safe strategy because all but Beach were too slow to stay with most pass receivers on long bombs without that head start. But Collier chose to cross up the Colts by having the backs crowd the receivers at the line of scrimmage. That would take away the Colts' fine short passing game.

Jim Brown must wonder what a man has to do to win a title. Despite shattering nearly every NFL rushing record, the Cleveland star entered this game still looking for his first championship.

But how would they keep Baltimore from springing the long pass on them? First, they would concentrate on a pass rush, surprising the Colts with a few blitzes from the linebackers. If they could break through often enough, Unitas wouldn't have time to wait for his receivers to run long pass patterns. Secondly, Cleveland could make use of an unusual ally, the wind. In late December, brisk, cold winds often swept off Lake Erie and blew through the open-ended Cleveland stadium. Not even Unitas would find it easy to throw deep against that wind.

Sure enough, the wind was blowing at more than 20 miles an hour at game time, and the Baltimore offense sputtered like an engine trying to start on a freezing day. Cleveland's strategy worked perfectly in the first half, and Unitas seemed frustrated by the tight Cleveland pass coverage. The heroic work of the defense seemed wasted, however, as the Browns' offense made no ground against the Colts.

Then Cleveland quarterback Frank Ryan made the kind of mistake that his coach feared could sink his team. One of his passes was intercepted, and Baltimore launched a drive deep into Cleveland territory. After the drive finally stalled at the 19, the Colts sent in kicker Lou Michaels to try the field goal. But holder Bobby Boyd bobbled the snap from center, and Michaels had no chance to kick the ball straight. The Browns escaped to their locker room at half time tied 0 to 0.

With the wind at their backs for only the third quarter, the Browns knew they had to score quickly. Led by little-known tackle Jim Kanicki, the Browns stopped the Colt offense early in the second half. Baltimore punter Ron Gilburg then punted into the stiff wind. The kick traveled only 25 yards and gave Cleveland good field position. Although the Browns continued to have problems moving the ball, kicker Lou Groza was able to boot a wind-aided 43-yard field goal for a 3-0 lead.

Throughout the game, most fans were wondering when the Colts' offensive explosion would come. The explosion of points finally did arrive, but it was the Browns who provided the fireworks. Jim Brown ran to his left, broke through the blue-shirted Colts, and raced 46 yards to the Colt 18. Quarterback Ryan then moved to strike before the Colts could recover. He had noticed that the Colts were guarding Paul Warfield closely. That meant he would have to try his other wide receiver, Gary Collins.

Lou "The Toe" Groza

Collins faked a short pass pattern and then dashed for the end zone. Ryan's pass was on target, and the Browns were suddenly on top by 10 to 0.

With the Colts stunned and the wind still behind the Browns, Cleveland went back on the attack. Baltimore's defense broke down in the clutch again as a defensive back misread the Browns' formation. That left the middle clear for Collins. Catching a high floating pass in full stride, Collins scored again, this time from 42 yards away.

Still there was no answer from the Colt offense, and the Browns marched right back, storming to the Colt one before Baltimore finally stopped them. Hurling back Jim Brown three times from the goal line, they forced the Browns to settle for a Lou Groza field goal. That kept the Colts within three touchdowns at 20 to 0. Everyone knew that Johnny Unitas could pull off a late rally to win the game as he had often done before.

This wasn't to be Johnny's day, however. Cleveland got the ball back, and Ryan teamed up with Collins for an instant replay of their earlier touchdowns. Catching up with Ryan's soaring pass, he sped 51 yards for another touchdown, the final blow in Cleveland's 27-to-0 win.

Collins claimed the game's Most Valuable Player Award by catching five passes for 130 yards and three touchdowns. Steady Frank Ryan had chipped in with 206 passing yards, and Jim Brown had added 114 tough running yards. But it was the Browns' defense that could claim most of the credit for the win. Jim Kanicki had beaten lineman Jim Parker to put a strong pass rush on Unitas. The great Colt quarterback had passed for only 95 yards while throwing two interceptions. Finally, the worst rushing defense in the NFL had held the Colts to 82 yards on the ground.

Many fans had expected the scorekeeper to be kept busy keeping up with the Colt tallies. Instead, the Colts didn't put a point on the board! The Browns' leaky defense had shut down the mighty Colts when it counted the most.

The Colts had been ready for Jim Brown, and they had kept him out of the end zone all afternoon . . .

41

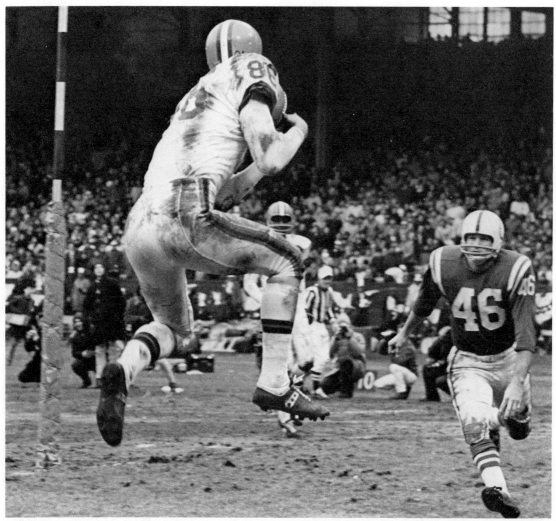

...but they had forgotten about Gary Collins, who had stolen the show from the more famous Baltimore receivers with three easy touchdown grabs, including this one in front of Baltimore's Jim Welch.

HOW THE BROWNS UPSET THE COLTS

December 27, 1964
Municipal Stadium, Cleveland
Attendance: 79,544

	Baltimore Colts	Cleveland Browns
1964 Record Prior to Game:	12-2	10-3-1
1964 All-Pros:	Bob Vogel (t)	Dick Schafrath (t)
	Jim Parker (g)	Paul Warfield (wr)
	Lenny Moore (rb)	Jim Brown (rb)
	John Unitas (qb)	
	Gino Marchetti (db)	
	Bob Boyd (db)	

	1	2	3	4	FINAL
Baltimore Colts	0	0	0	0	**0**
Cleveland Browns	0	0	17	10	**27**

Browns	Lou Groza	43-yard field goal
Browns	Gary Collins	18-yard pass from Frank Ryan (Lou Groza kick)
Browns	Gary Collins	42-yard pass from Frank Ryan (Lou Groza kick)
Browns	Lou Groza	10-yard field goal
Browns	Gary Collins	51-yard pass from Frank Ryan (Lou Groza kick)

		Colts	Browns
First Downs		11	20
Yardage:	Rushing	92	142
	Passing	89	197
	Total	181	339
	Penalized	48	59
Passing:	Completions	12	11
	Attempts	20	18
	Interceptions	2	1
Fumbles Lost		2	0

Outstanding Performance: Brown wide receiver Gary Collins caught five passes for 130 yards and three touchdowns.

Subpar Performance: Colt quarterback Johnny Unitas completed only 12 of 20 passes for 95 yards, two interceptions, and no touchdowns.

Fred Miller (76) and the rest of the powerful Colts could hardly wait to stuff Joe Namath's outrageous prediction down his throat.

★★★ 5 ★★★
Broadway Joe's Super Upset

New York Jets vs. Baltimore Colts
January 12, 1969

It was like a prisoner flashing the victory sign on his way to face a firing squad. Joe Namath's guarantee of a victory for his New York Jets over the Baltimore Colts in football's third Super Bowl was ridiculous.

The Colts represented the National Football League, and the past two Super Bowls had shown that league to be superior to the American Football League. Neither of the AFL champs, Kansas City or Oakland, had been able to give the NFL champion Green Bay Packers a close game in Super Bowl action. Evidence seemed to show the difference between the opponents for the 1969 Super Bowl was even greater.

The New York Jets had not overwhelmed their opponents in winning the AFL crown. They had won 11 and lost 3. Then they had nosed out Oakland in the title game, 27-23. Only three of their players were considered good enough to get on the league's All-Pro squad: quarterback Namath, pass receiver George Sauer, and defensive end Gerry Philbin.

The Baltimore Colts, meanwhile, appeared a notch stronger than the Packers had been. They had breezed through their season with a 13-1 mark and had trampled the Cleveland Browns, 34-0, in the title game. Their defense was led by hard-hitting linebacker Mike Curtis, huge defensive lineman Bubba Smith, and cagey defensive back Bob Boyd. Featuring an eight-man blitz that sent rival quarterbacks diving for cover, the Colts had allowed only 144 points and had posted 3 shutouts.

45

The Jets had never faced a battering ram like Baltimore's John Mackey.

Offensively, quarterback Earl Morrall had done a splendid job filling in for injured star Johnny Unitas. With offensive weapons such as tight end John Mackey and running back Tom Matte, the Colts had impressed everyone. Everyone but the Jets, that is.

The Colts started out in the Super Bowl as expected. They pushed the ball downfield so easily that it was as if they had the Jets outnumbered, two to one. Their offense had moved so well that it didn't seem important when place-kicker Lou Michaels missed an easy 27-yard field goal. The Baltimore defense was picking the Jets clean as they recovered a fumble on the Jets' 12-yard line. A score seemed certain when the Colts' Willie Richardson beat Randy Beverly on a pass pattern in the end zone. But Morrall's pass was tipped at the last instant and wound up in Beverly's hands for an interception. The Colts, who would have been ahead 10 to 0, were still without a score.

Colt fans could hardly wait to see their team bury Joe Namath under their all-out blitz. But the Jets, who normally relied on passing plays, had switched strategies for the Super Bowl. Instead,

Instead of the expected aerial duel, Super Bowl fans were treated to a ground war between two hard-nosed number 41s, New York's Matt Snell (left) and Baltimore's Tom Matte (right).

they used a 220-pound battering ram named Matt Snell. Behind the pounding blocks of left tackle Winston Hill, Snell charged ahead for steady gains on the surprised Colts. When Namath did pass, he beat the blitz with quick tosses to Sauer. The Jets slowly moved downfield from their own 20-yard line. Snell finished the job with a 4-yard burst into the end zone for a touchdown.

Snell takes a handoff from Namath while unsung hero Winston Hill (75) caves in the whole right side of the Colt line.

After the teams traded field goals, the Colts recovered from their surprise and began to strike back. Tom Matte tore through the arms of Jet defenders at the line of scrimmage and dashed into the open field. By the time the Jets caught up with him and hauled him down, Matte had run 58 yards to the New York 18-yard line. But Morrall wasted yet another scoring chance when he threw another interception— this time to a diving Johnny Sample at the two.

Although frustrated by their mistakes, the Colts continued on the attack. They turned back the Jets' offense and marched the ball back into scoring position. This time, they called for a trick play. Morrall gave the ball to Matte who ran, stopped, and tossed it back to Morrall. The Colt quarterback then looked downfield for an open target. The play had fooled the Jets so badly that wide receiver Jimmy Orr was completely alone in the end zone. He jumped and waved his hands, but somehow his quarterback didn't see him.

Morrall threw to the other side of the field where a Jet intercepted for a third time! At the very least, the Colts should have had 20 points on the board. But they headed for the locker room trailing 7 to 0.

Smoldering from their embarrassment, Baltimore charged out of the locker room for the second half. They were determined to dispose of the upstart Jets and their boasting quarterback. It was important for them to drive downfield and *score* on their first possession. That would take the fight out of the Jets, and then they could hammer them all over the field, as they were expected to do.

Sure enough, the Colts opened a large hole for Matte on the first play of the half, and he ran for nine yards. But disaster struck as Matte fumbled the ball. New York linebacker Ralph Baker recovered on the Colt 33, and Namath was able to inch his team close enough for a field goal by Jim Turner.

Suddenly behind, 10-0, it was the Colts who started floundering. They failed to make a first down the next time they had the ball, and they were forced to punt. Namath's quick passes then moved the Jets in range for another Turner field goal that put New York ahead, 13-0.

The proud Colts realized the game was getting out of control. Morrall had suffered through a terrible afternoon. He had completed only 6 of 17 passes, and 3 had been intercepted. The decision was made to call in the old miracle-worker, Johnny Unitas. Due to his arm injury, Johnny U had thrown only 32 passes all season, and he still wasn't able to throw the ball deep. A healthy Unitas might have been able to turn the game around, but a rusty, sore-armed Unitas could not. After forcing another punt, the Jets drove into Colt territory again. Snell continued to grind out tough yards, and Namath continued to go to Sauer with his quick tosses. A long pass to Sauer set up yet another Turner field goal, this one an easy try from within the shadow of the goal line. Turner then missed a chance to boost the lead to 19 points when his next attempt, a 42-yarder, failed to clear the uprights.

Late in the fourth quarter, Unitas finally brought the numbed Colts back to life. Helped by a rash of penalties on the overexcited Jets' defense, Balti-more finally scored a touchdown. They then recovered an on-side kickoff in Jet territory. Were the Colts going to pull off a dramatic comeback? The Jets answered that question with a firm "No." Four straight passes from Unitas fell incomplete, and the Jets took over. Baltimore had no more hope of winning. They could only watch in bewilderment as the Jets used up most of the remaining time with safe running plays.

The Jets had earned their 16-7 win with great performances from key players. Winston Hill had single-handedly controlled the line of scrimmage with his blocking. Namath had completed 17 of 28 passes. Snell had massed 121 yards on his runs. The defensive backs had come up with four key interceptions. With help from a few lucky breaks and miserable games by Colts such as Morrall, kicker Michaels, and defensive end Ordell Braase, the Jets had backed up Namath's guarantee of a victory. Although the Jets tried to claim that their win should have been no surprise, it truly was the most dramatic upset in NFL history.

HOW THE JETS UPSET THE COLTS

January 12, 1969
Orange Bowl, Miami
Attendance: 75,377

	Baltimore Colts	New York Jets
1968 Record Prior to Game:	13-1	11-3
1968 All-Pros:	John Mackey (te) Bob Vogel (t) Earl Morrall (qb) Mike Curtis (lb) Bob Boyd (db) Dick Volk (db)	George Sauer (wr) Joe Namath (qb) Gerry Philbin (de)

	1	2	3	4	FINAL
New York Jets	0	7	6	3	**16**
Baltimore Colts	0	0	0	7	**7**

Jets	Matt Snell	4-yard run (Jim Turner kick)
Jets	Jim Turner	32-yard field goal
Jets	Jim Turner	30-yard field goal
Jets	Jim Turner	9-yard field goal
Colts	Jerry Hill	1-yard run (Lou Michaels kick)

		Jets	Colts
First Downs		21	18
Yardage:	Rushing	142	143
	Passing	195	181
	Total	337	324
	Penalized	23	28
Passing:	Completions	17	17
	Attempts	29	41
	Interceptions	0	4
Fumbles Lost		1	1

Outstanding Performances: Jet quarterback Joe Namath completed 17 of 29 passes for 195 yards and no interceptions. Jet fullback Matt Snell ran for 121 yards in 30 carries and one touchdown.

Subpar Performance: Colt quarterback Earl Morrall completed only 6 of 17 passes for 71 yards, three interceptions, and no touchdowns.

Against Pittsburgh's Steel Curtain, Steve Grogan's task of rebuilding New England's team from patsies to Patriots seemed doomed.

★★★ **6** ★★★
Rebirth of the Patriots

New England Patriots vs. Pittsburgh Steelers
September 26, 1976

The New England Patriots spread gifts and brought good cheer wherever they went in 1975—at least for their opponents. In losing 11 of 14 games, the Patriots had made it easy for their foes with 43 fumbles and 28 pass interceptions. Not to be outdone, New England's defense chipped in with a whopping 103 penalties. With a pass defense that was riddled with holes and a pass offense that completed less than half of its tosses, they had been outscored 358 to 258.

It almost seemed as if the San Francisco 49ers had taken pity on the bumbling Patriots during the off-season. They astounded football buffs by trading three first-round draft choices, a second-round choice, and quarterback Tom Owen in exchange for Patriot quarterback Jim Plunkett. Plunkett, who had fallen victim to injuries, seemed to have lost most of the spark that had made him a college star. New England was able to replace him with Steve Grogan and to rebuild with draft choices such as defensive backs Mike Haynes and Tim Fox. Experts agreed that the extra draft picks gave the Patriots a good start on rebuilding and that they could be contenders again within a few years.

But few expected it would happen in 1976. Even after the Patriots stunned the Miami Dolphins, 30-14, to even their record at 1-1, no one took them seriously. New England was advised to enjoy the win while it lasted because next on the schedule was a trip to Pittsburgh. The Steelers had won two straight Super Bowl championships and looked like a good bet to take a third.

Nothing could have been worse for a team in need of confidence than a date with Steeler All-Pros such as defensive back Mel Blount (top left), tackle "Mean" Joe Greene (bottom left), and defensive end L. C. Greenwood (above).

From the raging fury of end Dwight White (above) to the ruthless efficiency of linebacker Jack Ham (right), the Steel Curtain had no weaknesses.

The Steeler defense struck fear into the hearts of most offensive units. Led by a long list of All-Pros such as Joe Greene, L.C. Greenwood, Dwight White, Jack Ham, Jack Lambert, and Mel Blount, Pittsburgh didn't care if their opponents ran or passed. In 1975, they had allowed the fewest first downs rushing *and* passing in the AFC and had led their conference by giving up only 162 points.

With his acrobatic catches, Lynn Swann added a dash of elegance to the Pittsburgh team.

Lately, they were finishing construction on an offense that was just as overpowering. Fullback Franco Harris had gained 1,246 yards in 1975. Quarterback Lynn Swann could catch passes so brilliantly that he had easily won the Most Valuable Player Award in the last Super Bowl. The only thing worse than having to play the Steelers was having to play them at Pittsburgh!

The game started with the champs calmly going about their business. Acting as if it were no more difficult than peeling an orange, they drove to the New England three. From there, reliable Franco Harris burst over for the touchdown. With the awesome Steeler defense spurred on by their home fans, a 7-point lead was the equal of a 20-point lead for most teams. This was especially true since New England had only second-year man Steve Grogan at quarterback. Only a fifth-round draft choice, Steve had impressed coaches with his strong running and strong arm, but he had a lot to learn about the pro game. Like most quarterbacks, Grogan had a miserable time trying to throw against Pittsburgh in the first half.

Fortunately for New England, the Steelers carried the ball as if it were covered with slime. Fumble after fumble fell into Patriot hands just as the Steelers threatened to run away with the contest. With their offense stopped cold, New England's attack consisted mainly of kicking to the Steelers and recovering their fumbles! Pittsburgh fumbled six times in the half, and New England turned three of those mistakes into John Smith field goals. The butter-fingered Steelers, meanwhile, could only answer with two field goals from Roy Gerela to hold a 13-9 halftime lead.

Having shaken the jitters, Pittsburgh pounded on the Patriots at the start of the second half. Harris raced 21 yards for a score to give them a commanding 20-9 lead. But the Patriots didn't panic. With such giants as John Hannah and Leon Gray anchoring the line, they were one of the few teams that could match the strength of the Steeler defensive line. With an unknown super athlete named Russ Francis at tight end and bruising Sam "Bam" Cunningham at fullback, New England could produce more power blocking than any team in the NFL.

New England unveiled a secret weapon, second-year man Russ Francis, who was just starting to emerge from the shadows after sitting out his senior year of college football.

Darryl Stingley's long scoring reception put the Steelers in a hole.

Grogan, who had hit only grass with his throws through most of the first half, suddenly got hot. Moving into Steeler territory, the Patriots unwrapped their secret weapon, Francis. Although Russ weighed 235 pounds, he could outrun nearly everyone on the field. The stunned Steelers looked on helplessly as the big guy raced past them to catch a 38-yard touchdown pass. The Patriots, back in the game, trailed only 20 to 16.

Rookie defensive backs Haynes and Fox were expected to provide Steeler quarterbacks Bradshaw and Swann with an easy afternoon of passing, but they played like cagey veterans. New England stopped Pittsburgh and sent their offense back on the field. This time, it was speedster Darryl Stingley who broke free for a big play. His touchdown catch and run covered 58 yards to put his team ahead, 23 to 20.

Grogan refused to cool off, and he marched his team down to the Steeler six. From there, the lanky star from Kansas State called his own number and scampered in for another touchdown. Suddenly, the Steelers were on the run, trailing 30 to 20.

Only when New England went back

to its old generous ways did the Steelers get back in the game. The Patriots fumbled on their 30, setting up a short touchdown toss from Bradshaw to tight end Randy Grossman. Pressured by an enraged Steeler defense, New England then had to punt again with 1:42 left.

If the Steelers expected the Patriots to cave in at the finish, they were sadly disappointed. Instead, it was Pittsburgh who bobbled the ball and committed a penalty. The Steelers frantically clawed their way close enough for Roy Gerela to try a 48-yard field goal with three seconds left. But the kick failed, and New England ran off with a thrilling, come-from behind win: 30 to 27.

By gaining 399 yards on the Steelers, New England had made fans sit up and take notice. With great performances from NFL Rookie of the Year Haynes and Francis, the Patriots went on to post an 11-3 mark to win a play-off spot. There it took a couple of controversial calls to help eventual champion Oakland squeak past them. It turned out to be a splendid year, and it could all be traced back to the game when the upstart Patriots wrestled a win away from the Steelers at Three Rivers Stadium.

New England hit the jackpot with their rookies, including super-smooth defensive back Mike Haynes.

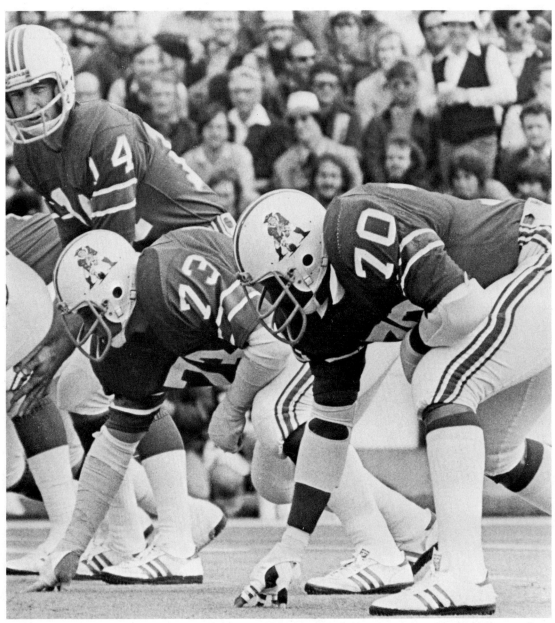

After feeling their muscle against the Steelers, Patriot linemen John Hannah (73) and Leon Gray (70) nearly pounded their way to a Super Bowl.

HOW THE PATRIOTS UPSET THE STEELERS

September 26, 1976
Three Rivers Stadium, Pittsburgh
Attendance: 47,379

	Pittsburgh Steelers	New England Patriots
Previous Year's Record:	12-2	3-11
Returning All-Pros:	Lynn Swann (wr)	None
	L. C. Greenwood (de)	
	Jack Lambert (lb)	
	Jack Ham (lb)	
	Andy Russell (lb)	
	Mel Blount (db)	

	1	2	3	4	FINAL
New England Patriots	6	3	14	7	**30**
Pittsburgh Steelers	7	6	7	7	**27**

Steelers	Franco Harris	3-yard run (Roy Gerela kick)
Patriots	John Smith	42-yard field goal
Patriots	John Smith	40-yard field goal
Steelers	Roy Gerela	32-yard field goal
Patriots	John Smith	26-yard field goal
Steelers	Roy Gerela	41-yard field goal
Steelers	Franco Harris	21-yard run (Roy Gerela kick)
Patriots	Russ Francis	38-yard pass from Steve Grogan (John Smith kick)
Patriots	Darryl Stingley	58-yard pass from Steve Grogan (John Smith kick)
Patriots	Steve Grogan	6-yard run (John Smith kick)
Steelers	Randy Grossman	11-yard pass from Terry Bradshaw (Roy Gerela kick)

		Patriots	Steelers
First Downs		18	24
Yardage:	Rushing	142	122
	Passing	257	281
	Total	399	403
	Penalized	52	70
Passing:	Completions	13	20
	Attempts	32	39
	Interceptions	2	0
Fumbles Lost		2	6

Outstanding Performance: Patriot tight end Russ Francis caught six passes for 139 yards and one touchdown.

Subpar Performance: The Steeler backs fumbled seven times and only recovered one of them.

After losing almost their entire offense, Houston's chances of beating San Diego in the play-offs hung by a thread. Here Lydell Mitchell slips through Vernon Perry's fingers to score a third-quarter touchdown for the Chargers.

★★★ 7 ★★★
Call Out the Reserves

Houston Oilers vs. San Diego Chargers
December 29, 1979

The second round of the 1979 play-offs featured a fascinating matchup of opposites. The Houston Oilers, with the NFL's most punishing running attack, were to take on the explosive passing offense of the San Diego Chargers in a contest of brute strength against speed and cunning.

When Houston showed up for the shoot-out, however, they left their weapons behind. The Chargers could hardly believe their good fortune when all three Oiler offensive threats were knocked out of action in Houston's first-round win over Denver! Earl Campbell, Dan Pastorini, and Ken Burroughs were the three men who could not be replaced in the Oiler offense. Somehow, they would now have to replace all three.

The biggest loss was running back Campbell. The second-year pro from the University of Texas had trampled the finest defenses in the league. Earl carried most of the load in Coach Bum Phillips' ball-control offense. Even with defenses knowing he would run most of the plays, Earl still averaged over 4.6 yards per carry and broke through for 19 touchdowns. In the play-off game against Denver, Campbell had barged into the end zone for a first-half touchdown when the ball popped loose. Not realizing he had already scored, Earl went after the ball and received a hard hit on his thigh. The injury put him out of that contest and the San Diego game.

The same half also cost the Oilers the services of wide receiver Ken Burrough. The speedy Burrough was the only long-pass threat the Oilers had to keep defenses from crowding the line of scrimmage.

The key to beating Houston was stopping Earl Campbell. The Denver Broncos had already done that for the Chargers by sidelining Earl with a deep knee bruise.

Finally, the Denver defense had forced Oiler quarterback Dan Pastorini to the sidelines. Houston had counted heavily on Dan staying healthy during the year. With only inexperienced reserve Gifford Neilson to take over, Dan's leadership would be sorely missed. The Oiler injury jinx continued into the week. Campbell's back-up at running back, Rob Carpenter, tripped over a blocking dummy during practice. Just two days before the game, he was hobbling around on crutches.

That left Houston with almost no way of challenging the Chargers' famous air attack. San Diego coach Don Coryell had designed a deadly passing offense, which was ably led by quarterback Dan Fouts. Known for his quick throwing motion, Fouts had gained over 4,000 yards passing during the year, more than anyone else in NFL history had accomplished in a season. With a variety of targets such as Charlie Joiner, John Jefferson, Bob Klein, and Lydell Mitchell, Fouts could usually find an open man. And with giant blockers such as Ed White and Russ Washington protecting him, he usually had plenty of time to look over the field.

Meet the crew of San Diego's Air Coryell: Pilot Dan Fouts (above), co-pilot John Jefferson (top left), and flight engineer Don Coryell (bottom left).

How did Robert Brazile and his teammates happen to always be in the right place at the right time?

Led by lineman Elvin Bethea, linebacker Robert Brazile, and the league's top interceptor, Mike Reinfeldt, the Oilers had put together a sound defense. But they could not hope to shut out the Chargers. Somehow the Oiler benchwarmers would have to get points against San Diego's fierce front four of Gary Johnson, Fred Dean, Louis Kelcher, and Leroy Jones. The experts didn't see much hope for that and made

Houston eight-point under-dogs.

The confident Chargers began firing from the start and moved quickly downfield. With Clarence Williams blasting over from the one, they sped off to a 7-0 first-quarter lead. But up in the Oiler press box, a pair of eyes was gaining valuable information. San Diego sent in their offensive plays with hand signals from the sidelines. Houston had figured out those signals and were relaying the information to defensive captain Gregg Bingham. He, in turn, put the Oilers in the right defensive formation to best stop the play.

Late in the first quarter, San Diego drove downfield again. This time Houston safety Vernon Perry happened to be in the right spot to intercept a pass at the Oiler 18. Since being cut by the Chicago Bears back in 1976, Perry had played in the Canadian Football League. Now in his first NFL season, Perry was not a familiar name to most American fans. But by the end of the afternoon, he would be.

The crippled Houston offense struggled as expected, and San Diego went on the attack once more. They moved deep into Houston territory during the second quarter and sent in Mike Wood to try a short field goal. The 26-yard kick would give them a 10-0 lead. Without an experienced quarterback to direct a strong passing game, it would be next to impossible for the Oilers to catch up. But Vernon Perry rushed in to block the kick. Scooping up the ball on the run, he raced all the way to the San Diego 15. Again, the Oiler subs could not move the ball, and they had to settle for a field goal from Toni Fritsch.

The lead held until the final minute of the first half. Following another interception by Perry, the Oiler subs did a valiant job. Rob Carpenter, who was in such pain that he had to crawl off the field at one point, battled for tough yards. Moving to within the shadow of the Charger goal line, the Oilers finally stalled and sent for Toni Fritsch again. In their haste to block the kick, the Chargers had sent 12 men onto the field. The resulting penalty gave Houston another chance, and fullback Boobie Clark ran around his left end for his only score of the season.

All of this, however, seemed like a minor nuisance to the high-powered San Diego club. Using a variety of receivers to pick apart the Oiler defense, Fouts moved to the Oiler eight in the third quarter. From there, Lydell Mitchell scooted into the end zone to put his team back on top, 14-10.

Late in that same quarter, Oiler receiver Mike Renfro trotted out, hoping to catch his first pass of the day. Slipping tackles and weaving through the San Diego defense, Renfro turned a routine short pass into a 47-yard touchdown romp! Charger fans began to get nervous as their team went into the final period trailing by three.

By now, San Diego should have learned not to tangle with Vernon Perry. But they hadn't, and the rookie seemed to snatch everything that came his way. It was fitting that Fouts' last toss, with two seconds to go, ended up in Perry's hands at the Oiler 27. Vernon's fourth interception of the day, a play-off record, sealed the Oilers' 17-to-14 win.

Passing for 380 yards, the Chargers had outgained their rival 380 to 259 and had been forced to punt only twice. The Oilers had, indeed, missed Campbell, Pastorini, and Burrough, but they still had had the only player they really needed—the incredible Vernon Perry!

All day, the ball had been bouncing right for Vernon Perry (32). This block of a Mike Wood field-goal attempt, which Perry returned for 56 yards, had made the difference in a three-point Oiler win.

HOW THE OILERS UPSET THE CHARGERS

December 29, 1979
Jack Murphy Stadium, San Diego
Attendance: 51,192

	San Diego Chargers	Houston Oilers
1979 Regular Season Record:	12-4	11-5
1979 All-Pros:	John Jefferson (wr) Dan Fouts (qb)	Earl Campbell (rb) - injured Robert Brazile

	1	2	3	4	FINAL
Houston Oilers	0	10	7	0	**17**
San Diego Chargers	7	0	7	0	**14**

Chargers	Clarence Williams	1-yard run (Mike Wood kick)
Houston	Toni Fritsch	26-yard field goal
Houston	Boobie Clark	1-yard run (Toni Fritsch kick)
Chargers	Lydell Mitchell	8-yard run (Mike Wood kick)
Houston	Mike Renfro	47-yard pass from Gifford Neilson (Toni Fritsch kick)

		Oilers	Chargers
First Downs		15	25
Yardage:	Rushing	148	63
	Passing	111	317
	Total	259	380
	Penalized	45	30
Passing:	Completions	10	25
	Attempts	19	47
	Interceptions	1	5
Fumbles Lost		0	0

Outstanding Performance: Oiler safety Vernon Perry intercepted four passes and blocked a field goal.

Subpar Performance: Charger quarterback Dan Fouts threw five interceptions and no touchdown passes.

After plugging the leaks in their secondary with the likes of Ronnie Lott (42), the 49ers were eager for a chance to avenge their 45-point loss to the Cowboys.

★★★ 8 ★★★
One Good Rout Deserves Another

Dallas Cowboys vs. San Francisco 49ers
October 11, 1981

The arrival of the Dallas Cowboys on October 11, 1981, brought painful memories to the San Francisco 49ers and their fans. It had been only a year since the classy Cowboys had trampled the 49ers in the most ridiculous game of the 1980 season. The faces of the 49ers had glowed as red as the trim on their uniforms when they had fallen behind, 38-7, at halftime. The second half had been almost too painful to finish when Dallas pulled out to a 52-7 lead in the third quarter and finally won, 59-14.

Danny White had befuddled San Francisco's defense with four touchdown passes in setting a team record for points in a game. But the 49er offense was at least as much to blame, as they gave the ball away a total of 10 times on fumbles and interceptions!

No one expected this rematch to be anything like the first mismatch, but neither did they expect San Francisco to win. Although the 49ers had posted a 3-2 record so far in the year, they hadn't yet beat a winning team. How different were they from the outfit that had lost 10 of its last 13 games at the end of the previous year?

In an effort to improve, San Francisco had made many changes. Veteran middle linebacker Jack "Hacksaw" Reynolds had come over from the Rams to lead the defense. Rookies Ronnie Lott, Carlton Williamson, and Eric Wright had been signed to mend the NFL's worst defensive backfield, and Joe Montana had taken over at quarterback from Steve DeBerg. Best of all, pass-rushing demon Fred Dean had just arrived from San Diego,

71

Cowboy quarterback Danny White (right) and running back Tony Dorsett (left) expected to take turns fattening their statistics at the expense of the hapless 49ers.

ready to do battle. Still, the experts at *Sports Illustrated* magazine sized up all the switches and declared that the 49ers could expect another 6-10 mark this year.

The Cowboys, meanwhile, had put together another in an endless series of championship teams. The Cowboys were a good bet to gain their 15th play-off appearance in the last 16 years and were the favorite to take the NFC title. With a defense led by the bruising front four of Randy White, Ed "Too Tall" Jones, Harvey Martin, and John Dutton, Dallas' defense was as rugged as ever. The offensive players who had torn apart the 49ers the year before—quarterback White, All-Pro runner Tony Dorsett, and a host of fine linemen and receivers—were also ready to go.

San Francisco started where they had left off a year ago when "Famous" Amos Lawrence wasted no time in fumbling the opening kickoff. Fortunately for him, a teammate recovered. Catching the confident Cowboys off guard, the 49ers drove 61 yards for a score. Montana flipped a pass to Freddie Solomon from a yard away for a 7-0 lead. The big test, however, would be the defense.

The 49ers' new quarterback, Joe Montana, made sure things would be different this time.

Danny White saw many new 49ers, many of them from uncomfortably close range. The face he saw the most belonged to Fred Dean, who came crashing in on him when he tried to pass. When they were forced to punt, Dallas knew winning wouldn't be so easy this year.

With clever play selection by coach Bill Walsh, San Francisco put together another steady drive. Mixing runs and passes well, they scored again on a four-yard run by Paul Hofer. Before the first quarter had ended, the men in red had marched for a third touchdown. The big gun in the 49er attack had been wide receiver Solomon, who had caught 5 passes for 74 yards and surprised Dallas with an option pass for 25 more. Big Johnny Davis plunged over from the one, and San Francisco enjoyed a 21-to-0 lead.

The Dallas defense finally pulled themselves together in the second quarter, but not before Ray Wersching's field goal had raised the score to 24-0. San Francisco fans were going wild as their team actually had the Cowboys on the run. But this was no scared

San Francisco's short-yardage pile driver, Johnny Davis, slammed into the end zone for the 49ers' third score.

bunch of amateurs. Dallas turned to a trick play to get back into the game. Danny White pitched out to Drew Pearson, who then fired to fellow wide receiver Tony Hill. The play was good for 22 yards and a touchdown and closed the gap to 24-7. While Dallas then shut down the 49ers for the rest of the half, they failed to score again.

Still hanging in the game, Dallas had the 49ers pinned back at their own 22 in the third quarter. But just 35 seconds later, the bewildered Cowboys looked up and saw 14 points on the 49er side of the scoreboard! Picking on Cowboy rookie defensive back Everson Walls, Montana had connected with cagey receiver Dwight Clark for a 78-yard touchdown pass. Defensive back Ronnie Lott then finished off a miserable day for Danny White by intercepting Danny's pass and racing 41 yards for San Francisco's fifth touchdown. That was all for White, who had thrown two interceptions while passing for only 60 yards. Thanks to Fred Dean and his pass-rushing friends, his backup, Glenn Carano, had no better luck.

Dwight Clark (87) gave Everson Walls (24) fits in their initial meeting, which developed into a key rivalry.

75

A Fred Dean (74) pass rush can take all the fun out of throwing a football!

Only one question remained: Could San Francisco ring up the same humiliating score that Dallas had the year before? A fourth-quarter touchdown run by reserve running back Amos Lawrence brought them closer at 45 to 7. The defense then stopped Carano and got the ball back for the offense. The 49ers, having the time of their lives, pushed all the way to the Dallas 28. It was then that Cowboy defensive back Benny Barnes kept the disaster from getting out of hand. He picked up a 49er fumble and dashed 72 yards to the end zone to make the final score 45-14. Even with Barnes' effort, however, it was the worst Cowboy defeat in over 10 years.

The 49ers had many stars to thank. Joe Montana had completed 19 of 29 passes for 279 yards and no interceptions. Dwight Clark had covered 135 yards on just four catches, and Ronnie Lott had made the big defensive plays. But the game ball went to newcomer Fred Dean. By collecting two sacks and forcing another, he had scrambled the Cowboy passing attack.

On the other hand, the Dallas defeat was a team effort. Hacksaw Reynolds claimed he had never seen a Dallas

The rout of the Cowboys proved to the 49ers that head coach Bill Walsh knew what he was talking about.

team so lifeless. Perhaps that 59-14 victory of 1980 had been *too* easy.

The game established the 49ers as true title contenders. When San Francisco and Dallas met again, it was for the NFC title. Finally, they stopped making each other look silly. In a thrilling, well-played contest, San Francisco pulled out a 28-27 win on a late rally. To cap a season of stunning upsets that had begun with the 45-14 pasting of the Cowboys in October, the 49ers then went on to top Cincinnati in Super Bowl XVI.

As a pro, "Famous" Amos Lawrence never quite lived up to his nickname, but he had added a fourth-period touchdown to the stampede over the Cowboys.

HOW THE 49ERS UPSET THE COWBOYS

October 11, 1981
Candlestick Park, San Francisco
Attendance: 57,574

	Cowboys	49ers
Previous Year's Record:	12-4	6-10
1981 Record Going into Game:	4-1	3-2
1981 All-Pros:	Herb Scott (g)	Randy Cross (g)
	Tony Dorsett (rb)	Fred Dean (de)
	Rafael Septien (k)	
	Randy White (dt)	
	Ed Jones (de)	

	1	2	3	4	FINAL
Dallas Cowboys	0	7	0	7	**14**
San Francisco 49ers	21	3	14	7	**45**

49ers	Freddie Solomon	1-yard pass from Joe Montana (Ray Wersching kick)
49ers	Paul Hofer	4-yard run (Ray Wersching kick)
49ers	Johnny Davis	1-yard run (Ray Wersching kick)
Cowboys	Tony Hill	22-yard pass from Drew Pearson (Rafael Septien kick)
49ers	Dwight Clark	78-yard pass from Joe Montana (Ray Wersching kick)
49ers	Ronnie Lott	41-yard interception return (Ray Wersching kick)
49ers	Amos Lawrence	1-yard run (Ray Wersching kick)
Cowboys	Benny Barnes	72-yard fumble return (Rafael Septien kick)

		Cowboys	49ers
First Down		10	23
Yardage:	Rushing	83	150
	Passing	109	280
	Total	192	430
	Penalized	40	28
Passing:	Completions	12	20
	Attempts	29	33
	Interceptions	2	0
Fumbles Lost		2	1

Outstanding Performances: 49er quarterback Joe Montana completed 19 of 29 passes for 279 yards, two touchdowns, and no interceptions. 49er wide receiver Dwight Clark caught four passes for 135 yards.

Subpar Performances: Cowboy running back Tony Dorsett gained only 21 yards in nine carries. Cowboy quarterback Danny White was replaced after completing only 8 of 16 passes for 60 yards and two interceptions.

ACKNOWLEDGMENTS: The photographs are reproduced through the courtesy of: pp. 1, 26, 47 (left), 48, Vernon J. Biever; pp. 2, 31, 34, 42, 62, UPI/Bettmann Archive; pp. 6 (Bill Amatucci), 54, 55, 56 (Bill Amatucci), Pittsburgh Steelers; pp. 8-9, 20 (left), 23, Minnesota Vikings Football Club; pp.. 10, 12, 13 (top), 16, 38, 41, Pro Football Hall of Fame; p. 13 (bottom), Philadelphia Eagles; pp. 14 (© NFL), 15 (© NFL), 52 (© George Gojkovich), 70 (© Fred Matthes), National Football League Properties; p. 18, Richard J. Hannah; pp. 20 (right) (Vic Stein), 21 (right), Los Angeles Rams; p. 21 (left), New York Football Giants; p. 22, Chicago Bears; p. 24, Fred Anderson; p. 28 (left) (Vernon J. Biever), Green Bay Packers; pp. 28 (top & bottom right), 29 (top left & right), Detroit Lions; pp. 29 (right), 36, 37, 46, 47 (right), Baltimore Colts; p. 39, Cleveland Browns; p. 44, New York Jets Football Club; pp. 57, 58, 59 (Thomas J. Croke), 60, New England Patriots; pp. 64, 66, Houston Oilers; p. 65, San Diego Chargers; p. 68, AP/Wide World Photos; p. 72, Dallas Cowboys Football Club; pp. 73, 74, 75, 76, 77, 78, San Francisco 49ers. Front cover photograph: Dallas Cowboys Football Club (Ron Scribner). Back cover photographs: Vernon J. Biever (top left), San Diego Chargers (Sam Stone) (bottom left), San Francisco 49ers (right).